G000296018

this book

BELONGS TO

oh Yes WE DiD™

Printed by Amazon Italia Logistica S.r.l.
Torrazza Piemonte (TO), Italy

10263281R00069